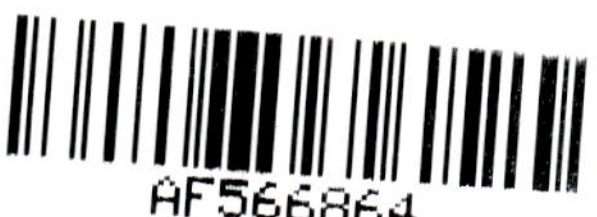

*table of contents*

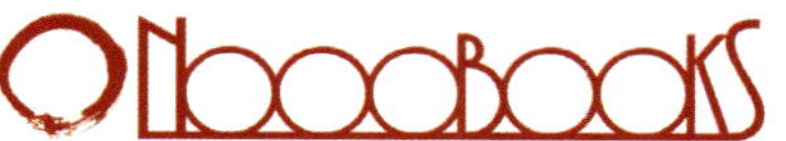